Firmly Planted

THE STORY OF THE
MORRIS ARBORETUM

THE
DONNING COMPANY
PUBLISHERS

John and Lydia
Morris as children.

Morris Arboretum of the
University of Pennsylvania
100 Northwestern Avenue
Philadelphia, PA 19118
(215) 247-5777
www.upenn.edu/morris

Arboretum contributors
Anthony Aiello
Robert Gutowski
Paul W. Meyer
Ann Rhoads
Kate Sullivan
Lauren K. Trax

The Donning Company Publishers
184 Business Park Drive, Suite 206
Virginia Beach, VA 23462

Steve Mull, *General Manager*
Jackie Trudel-Lane, *Project Director*
Dawn V. Kofroth, *Assistant General Manager*
Julia Kilmer-Buitrago, *Senior Staff Writer*
Sally Davis, *Editor*
Rick Vigenski, *Senior Graphic Designer*
John Harrell, *Imaging Artist*
Scott Rule, *Senior Marketing Coordinator*
Patricia Peterson, *Marketing Coordinator*

*Published with the support of the Malfer Foundation and the more than
6,000 member households of the Morris Arboretum.*

Library of Congress Cataloging-in-Publication Data
Available upon request
Printed in the United States of America.
ISBN No. 1–57864–139–X

Welcome to the MORRIS ARBORETUM!

Whether you're a first-time visitor discovering the glories of the garden, or a long-time member who was always curious about the origins of the Morris Arboretum, this book is for you.

The evolution of the Morris Arboretum from private estate to world-renowned public garden has taken more than a century, as many worthwhile things do. I remember when I first came to the Arboretum in 1975, it was still a sleepy, somewhat tattered but elegant garden, waiting to be awakened. I like to think we've accomplished a good deal of awakening, with much more work ahead.

Preservation of this revered space has been a constant effort, one that we perform gladly. We feel we are protecting an important resource as well as a piece of history. The plants that make up the living collection of the Arboretum are sometimes rare, sometimes unusual, but always significant historically and botanically.

Each time I walk through the Arboretum, even after twenty-five years, I discover something new. I hope you will return often to enjoy the beauty of each season, to discover its rich and diverse collection and to participate in the Arboretum's many programs.

Paul W. Meyer
THE F. OTTO HAAS DIRECTOR

John Morris.

Lydia Morris.

MISSION STATEMENT

The Morris Arboretum of the University of Pennsylvania is an historic public garden and educational institution. It promotes an understanding of the relationship between plants and people through programs that integrate science, art and the humanities. The Arboretum conducts four major activities: teaching, research, outreach and horticultural display. As the official arboretum of the Commonwealth of Pennsylvania, the Morris Arboretum provides research and outreach services to state agencies, community institutions and to citizens of Pennsylvania and beyond.

INTRODUCTION

As you explore and enjoy the Morris Arboretum, you experience a historic landscape full of ideas, diverse plants, and architectural forms, the art of design and the order of nature. How the Arboretum came to be is a question often asked. It is a story of plants and people in a garden.

The history of the Morris Arboretum has chapters in each of three centuries. It is the story of a private estate in the northwest corner of nineteenth-century Philadelphia that now begins the twenty-first century as a world-renowned public garden.

It is the personal story of the vision of a Quaker brother and sister who planted the seed of an idea to be cultivated by generations of stewards. Founders John and Lydia Morris planned and created a garden where art and science would thrive together and where stewardship would extend to caring for both plants and people.

The story is told in three parts.

It begins with Compton, the private estate established by John T. Morris and Lydia T. Morris with their purchase of farmland in 1887. They planted the first arboretum, built the buildings and planned for the creation of a school on the grounds.

The next chapter is the garden as the Morris Arboretum of the University of Pennsylvania, as established in the wills of John and Lydia. From 1933 to 1974, Penn's Botany Department developed the collection as a scientific collection, conducted academic research, and began formal and informal education programs.

The most recent chapter began in 1975. The Arboretum moved from the Botany Department to become an interdisciplinary center of the university combining programs in art, science, and the humanities. The mission was redefined, the first full-time director was hired, the Advisory Board expanded, and a master plan for restoration, renewal, and financial stability undertaken. The garden and programs today are the result of contributions by many individuals in each of these periods.

Throughout the garden is the collection, more than fourteen thousand curated and scientifically documented plants. There are stately trees planted by John Morris that are now regarded as champions for their size. There are young trees, wild-collected from North America, Asia, Africa and Europe that will be the garden treasures of the future. The collection helps us understand the plants that will green our cities and give beauty to our homes. There are seeds today in the greenhouses waiting to grow into plants that will be new to the garden world.

The structures in the garden also span the centuries. The Morrises not only designed many features themselves but also employed the finest local architects of their time. The knowledge that their garden is now on the National Register of Historic Places would have pleased John and Lydia, who were active in historic preservation. The Arboretum has also won recent recognition as one of the nation's best-designed public landscapes.

The education programs envisioned by the Morrises have blossomed. Each year, thousands of young students participate in school programs here. Interns from around the world participate in a year-long, professional development program. Each year, nearly one hundred classes are offered to adults and professionals. The Arboretum is the place to learn about trees and how to care for them.

Over seventy years of studying the plants of Pennsylvania has made the Arboretum the leader in information on the flora of the Commonwealth. Recent publications and a popular website help our botanical researchers deliver information to natural resource managers and advocates throughout the state and region.

The famous katsura tree growing on the grounds of Morris Arboretum began life as a small seed. Over time the tree grew, and its weight was supported by a variety of smaller trunks, each one responsible for upholding the plant grown from that one seed. In many ways, the life of the katsura tree is remarkably similar to the story of the Morris Arboretum. The seed was the idea for an Arboretum first contemplated by a plant-loving team of a brother and sister. Today the enormous responsibility of the Morris Arboretum is upheld by a sturdy group of dedicated men and women. Whether you are admiring the katsura tree or any other part of the Morris Arboretum, it is amazing how such a remarkable landmark grew from such a small idea that was firmly planted.

The early flower garden,
circa 1910s or early 1920s.

The Morris Mansion in 1967, the year before its demolition.

COMPTON
(THE PRIVATE ESTATE 1887–1932)

John Thompson Morris was born in 1847 to Isaac P. Morris, owner of I. P. Morris & Co. (later Port Richmond Iron Works) and his wife Rebecca. John's sister, Lydia Morris, was born in December 1849. Both children received the benefits of social standing and a strong educational background. When he was old enough, John Morris began to work for I. P. Morris & Co. in the manufacture of gears and shafts for ship engines. With his retirement in 1881, John Morris looked for other activities to occupy his time. In line with Victorian sentiments present at the time, wealth was not only measured in monetary assets, but in knowledge of the world and in philanthropic contributions to better the world. Because of their strong Quaker beliefs in stewardship of the earth, land preservation was a passion for both John and Lydia Morris. Not surprisingly, John Morris was the first president of the Chestnut Hill Horticultural Society in 1899. Both John and Lydia were also active in many city improvement committees. At one time John Morris was nicknamed the "champion of parks and playgrounds" for his extensive activities in urban renewal projects. One of his ideas was to extend Philadelphia's Fairmont Park to Fort Washington in Montgomery County.

John and Lydia Morris enjoying their gardens.

Various individuals felt the need to protect the land around Philadelphia from rapid city growth. With the advancement of the industrial revolution, urban sprawl began to be a large-scale problem. One of the more popular methods for reconnecting with their agrarian roots was for the wealthy to have summer homes in the country, surrounded by expansive and well-tended gardens or model farms. Indeed, while the Victorian era in America (1865–1914) was driven by the industrial revolution's focus on progress, this era also utilized the new technology to recapture remnants of its agrarian heritage. Improved greenhouses were home to a wide variety of exotic plants from around the world. The English idea of "gardens of pleasure" gained acceptance in America as an antidote to the growing urban decay. It was during this era that Central Park was designed to counter the massive growth found in New York City. Philadelphia city planners also began to set aside sections of Chestnut Hill as a retreat for wealthy residents.

In 1887, the Morrises purchased a sizable tract of twenty-six acres of farmland near the Wissahickon Creek for a summer home to replace their existing residence in the Frankford section of Philadelphia which was becoming industrialized and congested. Although designed to be a Victorian gentlemen's estate, John Morris felt his estate could be much more than a private pleasure ground. From the beginning, he and Lydia dreamed that someday it could become a public garden with a teaching and research mission and that the property should be an educational tool. In John Morris's own words, "I have no desire to make a large scientific collection, but as such, an exhibit as may have an educational value to the young people and those who will be helped to understand their surroundings intelligently."

The main building constructed by the Morrises was the mansion called Compton, designed by outstanding architect Theophilus P. Chandler, Jr. of Philadelphia in 1888. Compton was located on a hill overlooking the Wissahickon Valley and offered many views of the surrounding countryside through its stone arched windows. To the north, the windows at Compton provided a view of the Whitemarsh Valley. Much of the original landscaping was completed by Charles Miller, a landscape architect and Mt. Airy nurseryman who had been chief horticulturist for America's centennial celebration.

An early aerial view of the Rose Garden, circa 1920.

Lydia Morris in her Rose Garden at age seventy-nine in 1930.

Also built on the property was the carriage house, a structure designed to complement the main house. This massive stone building had wide carved dormers, picturesque window openings, and a slate roof. Its three levels were divided into distinct sections—the actual carriage house and stables for the horses and the storage of the Morrises' buggy (and later a sporty Pierce Arrow) and the attached employee residence.

Between 1892 and 1910, additional parcels of land were purchased from John Lowber Welsh adding 86.7 acres. As each section was added, additional garden features were designed. A Love Temple, Seven Arches, Step Fountain, Oak Allée, English Park, Japanese-influenced gardens that included the Overlook Garden, Hill and Water Garden and Fernery, and a classical Mercury Loggia became part of the landscape. The Morrises developed this eclectic Victorian landscape, drawing on a diversity of garden styles that they discovered through their readings and travels. Merged with the development of these garden features was a notable interest in assembling a labeled plant collection, that included native North American species, European plants, and most important, Asian species. The Morrises also valued authenticity in their gardens. For the construction of some of their Japanese gardens, the Morrises hired designers and gardeners from Japan. Eventually the grounds of the Morris Arboretum would cover more than 166 diversely designed acres.

Chestnut Hill was named for the American chestnut trees which once grew on the upper slopes along the Wissahickon Creek. The area around Chestnut Hill seemed to be an unlikely site for gardening. The land was rocky and sunburned and the hilltops subject to drought. The Morris Arboretum has portions of four major geological formations. The ridge on which Compton was located is formed of chickies quartzite, a highly resistant rock from about 550 million years ago. The weathering of this quartzite produces a sandy, acidic soil suitable for eastern red cedar, red, black and chestnut oak, dogwood, azalea, blueberry, hemlock, and sweet birch. Further down on the floodplain of the Wissahickon, the alluvial soil supports river birch, tulip tree, sycamore, boxelder, and spicebush. Wissahickon schist and gneiss underlie the area along Germantown Pike. The meadows along Paper Mill Run and on the farm occur on limestone formations characteristic of the Whitemarsh Valley to the northwest. Today, this diverse geology continues to provide a variety of habitats for the Arboretum's diverse plant collections.

Starting with John and Lydia Morris, and throughout its history as the Morris Arboretum, the plant collection has been comprised of a diversity of plants from around the northern temperate regions around the world. The Morrises, at the forefront of horticulture in their time, incorporated a large number of new and unusual plants into their landscape design. Having the luxury of a large gardening staff, they developed a Victorian landscape with intensively maintained and heavily planted gardens. Many of the Morrises' plants remain today, and these impressive specimens form the fabric and backdrop of the current garden.

Neither John nor Lydia ever married. They spent considerable time traveling throughout the world—from Europe to the Orient—collecting design ideas and unusual plants for display and research. Their first trip in 1881 was to England, France, and Italy. The second trip began in 1889 and took the Morrises around the world in eleven months. In 1894, the Morrises toured the Orient and collected a variety of specimens. Finally, the Morrises toured England, France, Italy, Spain, Russia, and Norway in trips during 1900, 1903, and 1906.

John Morris communicated with and traded plants with some of the leading plant explorers of his time, and plants in the Morrises' gardens were some of the earliest introductions of these newly discovered species in North America. One of his main contacts was Charles S. Sargent, first director of the Arnold Arboretum. Other contacts included British horticulturist Vicary Gibbs, nurseryman and writer Thomas Meehan, plant explorer David Fairchild (who later wanted his son to be a student at the Morrises' botany school), and plantsman E. H. Wilson. Together these plant enthusiasts would help to supply more than thirty-five hundred kinds of woody plants from around the world.

This view from 1926 shows the Rose Garden planted entirely in pansies.

The Fernery in 1900. Note the rounded glass panes of the roof.

The Fernery (circa 1980) after the first renovation. Note the straight slanted roof line.

The Fernery during renovation in 1994.

As time went by, specialized structures were built to add a sense of eclectic ambiance to the gardens. One dream of John Morris was to build a specialized greenhouse called a "fernery" to house varieties of ferns from around the world. John Morris designed an elegant structure with curved glass panes. The Fernery, built in 1899, was an irregular octagon measuring forty-three feet by thirty-four feet with seven feet of the stone wall below ground and approximately two and one-half feet above ground. Once his design was completed, John Morris submitted the architectural sketches to the British engineering firm of Lord and Burnham. After reviewing the plans, Lord and Burnham told John Morris bluntly that his design would never work. Undaunted by the rejection of his idea, John Morris hired Lord and Burnham's competition, Hitchings and Company, to build the Fernery according to his original plans. Contrary to the "professional opinion," the Fernery stood as an interesting display of architectural style without renovation for more than fifty years. Morris' engineering genius is shown through the successful use of roof braces which bore the weight of the glass and metal framing without having interior support poles.

In 1908, John Morris ordered construction of a Log Cabin for Lydia's private retreat. The building was constructed by Pugh and Hubbard of Philadelphia for the sum of $1,740.64, paid entirely in cash by John Morris. The Log Cabin was one of Lydia's favorite retreats and served as a reception area to serve tea and cookies on a fine silver tea set. Although rustic in appearance from the outside, the interior was well furnished with antiques.

The Log Cabin was not the first structure designed by John Morris for the grounds. In 1904 a lodge at Hillcrest Avenue and a Stone Bridge at the Swan Pond were constructed from John Morris' plans. Seven Arches was built from his design in 1911.

In 1913, another building ordered by John Morris was completed. The Mercury Loggia was built to commemorate the Morris' twenty-fifth anniversary at Compton. In a time capsule in the cornerstone is the "record commemorating the 25th Anniversary of our homecoming" according to John Morris. It is titled "Recollections associated with the Happy Home of John T. Morris and his sister Lydia T. Morris."

John Morris died in 1915, leaving the substantial property in trust to Lydia through the Pennsylvania Company for Insurance on Lives and Granting Annuities with a stipulation that she work to make Compton and the surrounding gardens into a botanical garden, horticulture museum, and school. According to John Morris' will, the Compton property should be a place "where young men and possibly young women may be taught practical gardening and horticulture, with a special view on practical work rather than the study of the scientific side of horticulture."

Lydia Morris moved permanently to Compton in 1915 to accomplish the goals set forth in John's will, but also added a "woman's touch" to the gardens. As manager of the estate, Lydia helped to create a "gentlewoman's garden" using flowering plants that she described as "fragrant with bloom" including lilacs, roses, and wildflowers that were "rich in color and graceful in simplicity." Additionally, Lydia Morris maintained a fruit orchard, vegetable garden, and areas for dairy cattle, pigs, and chickens to keep the estate self-sufficient.

To help fulfill the terms of John's will, Lydia began negotiations with Edgar V. Seeler in December of 1916 to build a school on the Bloomfield property and make the ancestral family summer home of Cedar Grove into a museum. Cedar Grove, the original summer house, stood in the Harrowgate section near Frankford and had been the summer home of five generations of the Paschall and Morris families. The Cedar Grove home was dismantled piece by piece and moved to Fairmont Park to become a Morris Museum, filled with family heirlooms and antiques.

Not everyone felt that another botanical garden was the best use for the property. Charles Sargent wrote his feelings to Lydia Morris in 1917: "It is my opinion that the establishment of a botanical garden (is) not necessary at this time. What is needed is to carry out the second paragraph of Mr. Morris' will which provides for the establishment and maintenance of a trade school for horticulture." Regardless, Lydia Morris continued with plans for both the school and botanical gardens.

Fernery, exterior, today.

The interior of the Fernery, circa 1980. Although the number of varieties of ferns had dwindled over the years, a wide variety of species still remained.

Fernery, interior, 1999.

A view of the Rose Garden and Compton, the Morrises' mansion, 1937.

The plans were completed in May of 1918 and included eleven Bloomfield drawings, a two-story academic building, water tower, dorm group, barn, greenhouses, and a power plant. The academic building and dorm group were to be located near the intersection of Stenton and Northwestern Avenues. The barn and greenhouses were going to be located where the present Horticulture Center now stands. Lastly, the power plant was to be located at the site of the old Springfield Mill on the banks of the Wissahickon. None of these projects was ever built.

Summerhouse in the corner of the Rose Garden in 1936.

The fireplace mantle in the Log Cabin as it appeared at the time of Lydia Morris.

The rustic Log Cabin was a favorite retreat of Lydia Morris.

The Log Cabin before renovation.

The Log Cabin after renovation.

In 1924, Lydia Morris approached the president of the University of Pennsylvania with an intriguing offer. At the time of her death, she suggested that the Compton property should be bequeathed to the University for use in education and botanical research as the Morris Botanical Garden, School, and Museum. Delighted with such an impressive offer, the president agreed. When Lydia died in 1932, the estate was left in trust to be administered by the University. The total estate at the time of Lydia Morris's death was valued at $4,000,000. With her generous donation, the Morris Arboretum of the University of Pennsylvania was founded with the purpose of furthering scientific research, botanical education, and horticultural display.

Research has always been an integral part of the mission of the Morris Arboretum. Pictured are Alfred Lisi (left), University of Pennsylvania Botany professor Dr. Harlan York (center), and an unnamed student conducting forest pathology research in the kitchen lab in the basement of Compton.

THE MORRIS ARBORETUM
OF THE UNIVERSITY OF PENNSYLVANIA
(1932–1974)

The terms laid out in Lydia Morris's will were quite specific. First, the areas of Compton and Bloomfield were to be maintained as an arboretum. Second, a laboratory was to be maintained for "botanical research and the dissemination of knowledge." Third, members of the Morris Arboretum were to conduct research not only in this country, but abroad as well. Fourth, a scholarship fund was to be founded for boys and girls interested in horticulture and similar subjects. Fifth, a postgraduate program was to be offered in horticulture or a related field. Sixth, the Morris Arboretum was supposed to publish books and pamphlets on the research work done at the Arboretum or other similar subjects. Seventh, the Arboretum was to employ "eminent scientific lecturers" to share their expertise with the public. Finally, Morris Arboretum was to provide a medium for the distribution of plants to the public.

The official opening ceremony of the Morris Arboretum of the University of Pennsylvania took place on June 2, 1933, with a gala event. Lectures, academic procession, orchestral music, an address by President Abbott Lawrence Lowell of Harvard, and the conference of honorary degrees were some of the activities of the day.

The first decade of the Morris Arboretum brought up many issues surrounding the actual implementation of Lydia Morris' will. Botany had always held a high place at the University of Pennsylvania, and the addition of the Arboretum was a tremendous gain. A report from Thomas Gates, president of the University of Pennsylvania in December 1932 described Morris Arboretum as a "broad and permanently significant creation, a dedication to the future of institutions and people . . . [an] unrestricted opportunity to make the most profitable social investment—an investment in inquiring and developing human minds."

Once the Arboretum became part of the University of Pennsylvania in 1932, the focus shifted from that of an aesthetic landscape garden to more of a research and collections based Arboretum. Plants in the garden at the time were arranged based on taxonomic relationships and often genera were planted together more for purposes of evaluation than for their integration into the landscape.

Dr. Rodney H. True was selected as the first director. Dr. H. H. York was hired as a specialist in plant diseases. Dr. Edgar T. Wherry and Dr. Conway Zirkle were hired as specialists in ecology and physiology, respectively. Finally, Dr. John M. Fogg, who later became director, took on the daunting task of taxonomist.

Cataloging the species of plants has always been a focus of the Morris Arboretum staff. The first secretary of the Living Collection at the time was Jane R. Heller who typed cards for each plant.

One of the top priorities for the Morris Arboretum committee was providing public access to the Arboretum. So in 1935, the Morris Arboretum began offering membership to the public. A quarterly publication, *The Arboretum Bulletin*, was begun that same year. Unlike scholarly journals, *The Arboretum Bulletin* was designed to cover a wide variety of topics for the botany and horticulture enthusiast. A lecture series began with experts from around the world as contributors.

As the activities offered at the Arboretum increased, it became quite clear that a curator was needed to handle the affairs of the facility. In 1940, Dr. Henry T. Skinner, who later became the director of the U.S. National Arboretum was selected for the first curator of Morris Arboretum. Dr. Skinner served in this position from 1940 to 1943 and from 1945 to 1952. Skinner brought to the Arboretum his experience and his passion for hybridizing hollies and deciduous azaleas. Among the duties listed for the curator were discriminating selection and determination of authenticity or identity of plants, creating a pleasing and artistic arrangement and skillful maintenance of gardens, protecting exhibits against deterioration and possible abuse, and fostering the enjoyment and educational benefits derived by the public from the collections.

SUSIE WALKER

Susie Walker was involved with the Arboretum for more than sixty years. For many years she served as president of the members' organization. Susie Walker also served on the Arboretum's board for two decades, including serving as chair of the public programs committee. An avid floriculturist, Susie Walker exhibited plants at the Philadelphia Flower Show and Chestnut Hill Flower Show. Among her greatest accomplishments was being awarded the Dorothy Falconer Platt Award of the Garden Club of Philadelphia. After her death in January of 2000, a purple leaf European beech tree was planted in her memory. One of her main areas of emphasis was education. Susie Walker started what is now the Morris Arboretum volunteer guides program in 1973 after seeing a need for guides. Known for her enthusiasm and optimism, Susie Walker received an award honoring twenty-five years of guide service in June of 1998. Endowments contributed in her memory help support the children's education programs.

Rock Wall, 1999.

F. OTTO HAAS

F. Otto Haas was named chairman of the Arboretum's Advisory Board of Managers in 1972. Otto Haas helped to guide the transfer of the Arboretum from the Botany Department of the University of Pennsylvania to the Provost's office. He was both well-liked and well-versed in scientific disciplines, having received his doctorate from Princeton University in organic chemistry. Otto Haas helped to formulate a long-term plan and worked to make certain that each goal set was reached. He helped to launch the First Century Campaign which raised $7 million in three years. Under the leadership of Dr. Haas a focus was made on revitalizing research programs, expanding teaching and outreach service programs, and converting historical buildings to laboratories and classrooms. Dr. Haas stepped down from his position as chair on June 12, 1989, but continued to be active until his death in 1994.

In addition to providing Board leadership, F. Otto Haas volunteered in the greenhouse.

Although the Arboretum was gaining recognition as a preeminent site for botanical education, time had begun to take a toll on some of the facilities. In 1941 the glass houses for palms and roses were both removed due to severe structural deterioration.

In 1948, the Arboretum and estate trustees purchased the Thayer property, a 3.5 acre property with a residence designed by famed architect Wilson Eyre built in 1893. This building was restored and dedicated as the Thomas Sovereign Gates Hall, named after the University of Pennsylvania president, with the purpose of providing suitable accommodations for the

MARION R. RIVINUS

Marion Rivinus was the first president of the Morris Arboretum Associates, a position she held from 1956 through 1967. Her other activities at Morris Arboretum included a position as member of the Advisory Board of Managers of the Morris Trust which she held until her death in 1981. The Rose Garden was rededicated as the Marion R. Rivinus Rose Garden in her honor in 1974.

administrative offices. Additionally, educational classes were held in the basement of Gates Hall.

The Fernery started to show signs of wear in the 1950s. By the mid-1950s, the structure was in disrepair and closed to the public. Starting in 1957 a stabilization project replaced the roof with a steel-supported frame and reglazed and replaced the curved glass panes with flat panes. This significantly changed the outward appearance of the Fernery from a rounded to an angular shape. Also at this time motorized vent controls were added to enhance the efficiency in temperature control. Once the Fernery stop-gap repairs were competed, each specimen was cataloged and inventoried. The total size of the collection had gone from four hundred specimens during John Morris' time to two hundred.

In 1954, Dr. John M. Fogg, Jr. took over the position as director at the Arboretum, a position he held until 1967. In writing about "Landscaping the Arboretum" in a 1965 *Morris Arboretum Bulletin*, Fogg referred to earlier planting design and captured the spirit of the planting concepts during this period when he wrote that, ". . . as often happens in large private estates, greater emphasis has been devoted to aesthetic values than to systematic or ecological relationships. Thus, coniferous and deciduous groups were promiscuously intermingled and honeysuckles, viburnums, lilacs, azaleas, maples, oaks, ashes, dogwoods, hollies, etc., were scattered in a hit-or-miss fashion throughout the grounds. The result, while often pleasing to the eye, was a far cry from the ideals of an arboretum which should not only be aesthetically satisfying but should seek to bring together . . . plants which are taxonomically related."

A map and brochure guide to the Arboretum from the early 1960s indicates the organization of plant groups as developed by Henry Skinner, Jack Fogg, and others. Plants were grouped together based on their cultural requirements and taxonomic relationships without attention paid to the effect on the historic fabric of the landscape. Although we no longer adhere to the planting concepts from this period, many of these older collections remain as significant components of the landscape and the core of some of the most important plant collections. The site below Gates Hall was immediately

The internship program attracts students from around the world.

Schoolchildren explore the Fernery with volunteer guide Joe Donahue.

High school students receive vocational training in arboriculture.

DR. ANN FOWLER RHOADS

Ann Rhoads has served as plant pathologist and botanist at the Morris Arboretum since 1976. In her early years, she launched an Integrated Pest management program at the Arboretum and more recently has led the Arboretum's flora of Pennsylvania research program. Through the program, all native and naturalized plants in Pennsylvania have been inventoried.

She is a recognized leader in the field of plant conservation and has received numerous awards including a Lifetime Achievement Award from the Girl Scouts of Pennsylvania for her work.

She is currently serving as senior botanist for the Arboretum. She co-authored "Plants of Pennsylvania: An Illustrated Manual" with her Arboretum colleague, Dr. Timothy Block in 2000. ❧

selected as being appropriate for growing hollies, and this collection was mostly planted in the late 1940s and early 1950s, resulting in the mature plants now seen. Additional hollies have been planted over the years and the Arboretum now has one of the largest holly collections in the country. Other core collections from this period are the Magnolia Slope, dogwoods along Wheelpump Road, witch hazels in the English Park, and the collection of Asian maples near the Overlook Garden.

It was during Fogg's tenure that the first credit courses were offered at the Arboretum, including plant taxonomy and field botany. Courses, lectures and tours for the public were also initiated.

One of the most influential people in the history of Morris Arboretum, Dr. F. Otto Haas, assumed the position of chair of the Advisory Board of Managers in 1972. A quick review of the Arboretum in the early 1970s showed a facility in need of substantial work. The Rose Garden was overgrown and had lost its recognition by the Rose

The Plants of Pennsylvania

AN ILLUSTRATED MANUAL

Ann F. Rhoads & Timothy A. Block
Illustrations by Anna Anisko

This 1,000+ page reference work written by two Arboretum botanists catalogues all the flora found in the Commonwealth of Pennsylvania.

Society. Historical architecture was crumbling or had been torn down completely. The Compton Mansion had been torn down in 1968 and the Log Cabin was boarded up to prevent vandalism and deterioration in 1969. The Living Collection was poorly curated and access to facilities and parking was limited. The "quiet years" at Morris Arboretum left a considerable amount of restoration needed from the new leadership.

A very northern population of Japanese camellia *(Camellia japonica)* in South Korea. Progeny from these plants are now the subject of a winter hardiness research study at the Arboretum and sister institutions.

THE MORRIS ARBORETUM
OF THE UNIVERSITY OF PENNSYLVANIA
(1975–PRESENT)

"More than a garden, more than a passive witness to history, the Morris Arboretum is involved in a widening circle of relationships that reach around the world. The interplay of an elegant garden and research and teaching excellence brings it before the public and at the same time provides a focus for the most scientific investigations—projects that may take years to pay off, but which ensure that our descendants will enjoy and use the Arboretum." (Dr. William M. Klein, First Century Campaign)

In 1975, the Morris Arboretum was transferred from the Botany Department to the guidance of the Provost's office as one of the University of Pennsylvania's Interdisciplinary Resource Centers. Research and educational programs were expanded to include plant introduction, integrated pest management and a renewed commitment to documenting and describing the flora of Pennsylvania.

Paul Meyer on a 1994 plant collecting trip in Hubei, China, with an important collection specimen, Paper Bark Maple *(Acer griseum)*.

Another significant achievement for the Morris Arboretum was brought about through the work of Dr. Edgar T. Wherry, an author of popular guides to ferns and wildflowers. An assistant professor of ecology at the University of Pennsylvania in 1930, Dr. Wherry remained active with the Morris Arboretum from 1932 until the mid-1970s. In 1979, the Morris Arboretum published an Atlas of the Flora of Pennsylvania based on the information compiled over almost fifty years by Dr. Wherry, Dr. Fogg, and Herbert A. Wahl.

Paul Meyer with Chinese scientists writing field notes on the 1997 NACPEC trip.

Throughout the 1970s the staff at Morris Arboretum continued to grow. In 1977, William McKinley Klein, Jr., was hired as the first full-time director. Klein, assisted by a new, young staff, launched into a comprehensive master planning effort with the Philadelphia planning firm Andropogon Associates.

A great honor was bestowed on the Morris Arboretum in 1978 with its inclusion on the National Register of Historic Places. With this significant designation, the Board took a serious look at the needs of the facility and grounds. A long-range program for renewal was adopted in 1978 with plans for restoration and the building of new facilities.

Dr. Ann Rhoads and Dr. Cui of Xian Botanic Garden, China, photograph plants in the New Jersey Pine Barrens.

Presentation of swans from the City of Ottawa to Philadelphia in 1982.

Swan Pond and Love Temple in winter.

WILLIAM MCKINLEY KLEIN, JR.

William Klein was director of the Arboretum through the years of great renewal and change between 1977 and 1991. Many credit William Klein with rescuing the Arboretum from extinction. Over the period of his employment the annual budget was raised from $300,000 to more than $2 million. He also convinced the legislature to designate Morris Arboretum as the Commonwealth of Pennsylvania's official arboretum. Dr. Klein received his bachelor's in range science forestry and his master's in botany from Colorado State University and finished doctoral work in botany at Claremont Graduate School. Among his greatest achievements were laying the foundations for the internship program and the master planning effort to revitalize Morris Arboretum.

One of the first new facilities under the long-range plan was the construction of the Horticulture Center. This horticulture facility provided an improved setting for support and freed the carriage house to be adaptively reused as the George D. Widener Education Center. The education center provided much-needed classrooms that, along with new staff, enabled the youth education, professional education and continuing education programs to grow and become significant resources.

The Swan Pond got new residents in the spring of 1982. Two swans were presented to the City of Philadelphia as a tercentenary gift from Ottawa, Ontario, Canada. The two swans, reminiscent of Lydia Morris's original swans Elsa and Lohengrin, were the latest addition in the long line of swans for the Swan Pond, a man-made pond built in 1904.

At the time of Morris Arboretum's centennial in 1987, there were thirty-four full-time staff, sixteen part-time staff, and an incredible three hundred fifty volunteers. The centennial year brought new recognition to the Arboretum as a cultural resource. A major grant from the National Endowment for the Humanities enabled the Arboretum to better interpret its rich heritage for visitors. One centennial event was the "Plants Under Glass" exhibit developed with the Royal Botanic Gardens, Kew. This was the central exhibit at that year's Philadelphia Flower Show; it also won the first Gold Medal awarded to a North American exhibitor at the Chelsea Flower Show.

On April 29, 1988, Governor Robert P. Casey signed House Bill 1071 into law which designated Morris Arboretum as the official arboretum of the Commonwealth of Pennsylvania. In the same year, Morris Arboretum began a collaborative effort with SmithKline Beecham into the research of medical substances found in the plants of Morris Arboretum's Living Collection.

In the 1990s the Log Cabin was restored. The eleven-foot by sixteen-foot Adirondack Mountain-style cabin with a cobblestone fireplace and chimney was composed of cedar logs and a pine floor. Among the areas upon which the restoration team focused were the missing wrap-around porch, collapsed piers, rotted timbers, and moss-sodden roof.

The Pump House was renovated in 1994, and the Rose Garden had been under continuous restoration since the 1970s. A 1-1/4 mile paved loop path completed in 1995 signaled the Arboretum's intent to make the institution accessible to all.

By the early 1970s many of the collections developed in the preceding decades had become unruly masses of plants overrun with excessive amounts of weedy invasive shrubs. These overgrown beds did not complement the original landscape design and one of the major curatorial tasks was to peel away the overgrown layers and expose the original vistas and collections that remained.

Historic sight lines, vistas, garden features, and garden areas were redefined and restored and plants were located in concert with these design concepts. Current planting practices take into account plants' cultural requirements while also maintaining the historic landscape. The result is a garden and aesthetic experience in which the scientifically-based plant collection is merged with the historic landscape.

As the process of redefining the garden continued, the Arboretum shifted its focus back to reinvigorating its plant collections. Many of the Arboretum's finest specimens like the lacebark elm and Engler beech probably originated from the plants the Morrises received from E. H. "Chinese" Wilson of the Arnold Arboretum. By the late 1970s it was clear these plants were aging and new plantings were needed. At that time, Director William Klein and Curator Paul Meyer made a commitment to rebuild the collection with wild-collected, scientifically documented plants. Currently, these plant collections give special emphasis to woody Asian species of landscape value and their native North American counterparts. Emphasis was placed on species representatives of known origin and special efforts were made to grow wild-collected species of documented origin. In cases where many selections have been made of popular, ornamental plants such as roses, magnolias, and crabapples, cultivated varieties which represent the best selections available are displayed. Several plant groups were identified as strengths and areas of focus: including firs, maples, magnolias, hollies, and members of the witch hazel family. Special attention was given to the acquisition of tree species that are well adapted to difficult urban sites.

Former Director of Horticulture/Curator Rick Lewandowski on a NACPEC trip to Shaanxi, China in 1996 with a fruiting specimen of *Paeonia obovata*.

Over the past twenty years, Arboretum curators have participated in expeditions with sister institutions to Korea, Taiwan, China, Pennyslvania, and the southern Appalachian Mountains. The Morris Arboretum is a founding member of the North American-China Plant Exploration Consortium (NACPEC). Significant plant groups from these expeditions include camellias (*Camellia japonica*) collected from the northernmost limit of their range in Korea, and several groups of kousa dogwoods (*Cornus kousa*) collected from northern South Korea and potentially among the most cold hardy of this species in the United States.

One of the main goals of NACPEC was to broaden the genetic pool of plants from both the United States and China. A wider genetic pool may result in increased cold hardiness, heat tolerance, overall vigor, and tolerance of stressful urban and suburban conditions. Other goals of NACPEC included the introduction of species with insect and disease resistance, conservation of rare species, selection of new garden forms, and introduction of new species. In the collection currently are more than five thousand plants of approximately nine hundred taxa that are of wild-collected origin. These plants include many unusual and rare species, seldom seen in cultivation in the United States.

By June of 2000, Morris Arboretum was home to more than 13,000 accessioned plants covering more than 2,400 taxa from 27 countries. Approximately 200 accessioned plants are added annually and kept in a computerized database.

The publication *Exotic Trees of New Jersey, Philadelphia and Metro New York* by Rutgers University's John E. Kuser included the Morris Arboretum as the institution with the largest number of non-native plants, which demonstrates the historic value of its plant collection. Some of the trees which helped Morris Arboretum win this distinction were the katsura tree (planted as a sapling in 1902), the tabletop Scotch elm (planted before 1909) and the weeping European beech (planted in 1909).

In 1993, the Morris Arboretum was the site of an International Symposium on the Utilization of Medicinal Plants, the first of its kind to be held in the United States.

The Pennsylvania Flora Project in the Arboretum's Botany Department maintains a database and website with information on all native and naturalized plants that grow in Pennsylvania. A 1993 book by Dr. Ann Rhoads and William M. Klein, "The Vascular Flora of Pennsylvania: Annotated Checklist and Atlas" showed distribution maps of all Pennsylvania plants. In spring, 2000, University of Pennsylvania Press published "The Plants of Pennsylvania: An Illustrated Manual" by Drs. Ann F. Rhoads and Timothy Block with artist Anna Anisko. This 1,000-plus page identification guide lists all the flora in the commonwealth.

PROGRAMS

John and Lydia Morris hoped to establish more than a garden of plants. They desired a public garden with strong education and museum programs. How well their idea was planted! Each year over 45,000 visitors come to the garden just to enjoy the beauty, most of these come with family and friends. There are an additional 40,000 participants in the many public programs offered to members and the general public. The Morris Arboretum is firmly planted as one of the region's most respected educational resources.

The Internship program offers graduate credit and a yearlong experience in professional development that attracts participants worldwide. Former interns have become educators and horticultural leaders nationwide.

Youth Education programs and school tours introduce young people to environmental themes in science, art, and humanities. Curricula are coordinated with state and local school standards. Nearly one hundred volunteer guides deliver the program and are deeply involved in program development and evaluation.

JANE JORDAN O'NEILL

Jane Jordan O'Neill was a valued member of the Arboretum community. She joined the Advisory Board of Managers in 1972. Among her positions were vice chair and chair of the Moonlight and Roses Committee and honorary chair of the Capital Campaign. She also was a generous Arboretum donor and played a key role in reversing its declining fortunes.

PAUL W. MEYER

Paul W. Meyer was appointed as the *F. Otto Haas Director* of the Morris Arboretum in 1991 and has held this prestigious position ever since. After graduating from Ohio State University and receiving his master's at the University of Delaware, Paul Meyer became curator of the Living Collection in 1976. Since 1979, he has traveled on eight plant-collecting expeditions to remote regions of China, Korea, and Taiwan.

As director he has led efforts to restore the public garden, stabilize Arboretum finances and strengthen its children's education and research programs. He is a founding member of the North America–China Plant Exploration Consortium (NACPEC).

Members and nonmembers choose from more than ninety continuing education courses offered at the Arboretum. Courses include birding trips, tree construction protection, landscape drawing, cottage gardening, healing herbs, and many others. There are classes for children, adults, and professionals.

Volunteering at the Arboretum is enjoyed by over five hundred community members serving as guides, gardeners, botanists, trustees, committee members, educators, hosts, and assistants of many kinds.

Outreach and Urban Forestry programs have helped over one thousand community groups in the last several years. Partnerships with state and federal agencies have extended programs nationwide. The Arboretum directed the nation's largest federally funded urban forestry program in a seven-year partnership with the USDA Forest Service. This program serving northeastern Pennsylvania won state, local, and national awards. The Arboretum is implementing a major restoration of the Paper Mill Run as a model for stream-bank management. This project is called the Paper Mill Run Riparian Corridor Restoration/Demonstration Project.

Events make the Morris Arboretum a special experience for friends and family with music and performing arts from many cultures presented out of doors with the garden as the theatre.

Some choose the Arboretum as a convenient and unique meeting place for their business or community group. Others choose the Arboretum as a very special place for a wedding or celebration.

The annual Spring Plant Sale is highly valued by members who find the best and the rarest of plants for their gardens, and receive a choice dividend plant propagated in the Arboretum greenhouses.

Moonlight and Roses, an annual dinner and celebratory Rose Garden season opener, is an opportunity for many members to share their enthusiasm for the Arboretum plants and programs.

All the Arboretum's programs are founded in the garden and its magnificent collection of plants. The growth and success of programs are fruit of the Morrises' firmly planted idea for a public garden based on stewardship and blending art and science.

Pump House before renovation. By the late 1970s, many of the Arboretum's features had become run-down and overgrown.

Pump House after restoration.

Lower meadows before the Entrance Drive.

The Entrance Drive, 1998.

Grotto underneath the Mercury Loggia is visible at the bottom of the photo.

Morris Arboretum provides a beautiful subject matter for artists.

For many visitors, the Morris Arboretum is a quiet place to spend time with family and friends. The stone bridge near the Wissahickon Creek is a favorite retreat.

Rose Garden entrance in 1999.

Summerhouse in the Rose Garden after restoration.

Rose Garden fountain.

Horticulturist Mike Tuszynski pruning in the Rose Garden.

Sculptures of John and Lydia Morris by Michael Price.

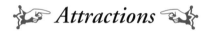

Attractions

DORRANCE H. HAMILTON FERNERY

One of the most interesting structures at Morris Arboretum, both in living content and architectural design, is the Fernery. Designed by John Morris, the Fernery was constructed of one hundred tons of local stone. After almost a century of deterioration with only one partial restoration effort, the Fernery was made one of the key areas for renovation in the early 1990s. With a $1.2 million price tag, the Fernery was one of the most extensive restoration projects at Morris Arboretum. After more than a year of work, the Fernery was rededicated as the Dorrance H. Hamilton Fernery on October 30, 1994. Today the Morris Arboretum has the only remaining free-standing Victorian estate fernery in North America. It houses numerous subtropical species of ferns and related plants.

ENGLISH PARK

One of the most noticeable features of the English Park which remains today is the Step Fountain. It was commissioned by Lydia Morris in 1916 in honor of her brother John who had died shortly before. It comes as no surprise that the fountain faces the mansion and would have been easily viewed from Compton's windows. After decades of deterioration, the Step Fountain was restored and a new sculpture "After B.K.S. Iyengar" installed in 1988.

GEORGE D. WIDENER EDUCATION CENTER

One of former Director William Klein's goals was to provide facilities for education on the Arboretum grounds. In 1982, the George D. Widener Education Center opened, replacing the existing classroom facilities at Gates Hall. The carriage house from the original estate was restored with a gift from the George D. Widener Foundation.

JAPANESE INFLUENCES

The impetus for the inclusion of a Japanese tea house and garden was fostered by the trips of John and Lydia Morris to the Orient in the 1890s. The tea house was commissioned by John Morris and constructed in Japan by local craftsmen. Once completed, the house was disassembled and sent to Philadelphia. The tea house was reconstructed at the Morris Arboretum in 1898. Mr. Sato, a Japanese gardener, was hired to create a garden to accompany the tea house. Tragically, neither the tea house nor its garden remain today, but surviving records give some description. The tea house was reached by a narrow stone-lined path which led into the woods from the top of the hill near the carriage house, now the Widener Visitor Center. Winding paths led through the garden which contained Japanese maple, bamboo, and a wide variety of azaleas. A water basin was located in the center of the garden for washing one's hands before entering the tea house.

In 1902, a landscape architect named Mr. Furikawa created a Japanese-style pond on the eastern edge of the property. This basin, lined with stonework and a mounded rockery on the eastside,

was surrounded by pines, Hinoki False Cypress, arborvitae, and cut-leaf Japanese maples. This remains next to the katsura tree at the base of the Holly Slope.

In 1905 another Japanese area was added to the Morris grounds. This time John Morris hired Mr. Muto, the architect of Fairmont Park's Japanese garden, to design a Hill and Water style garden. A Hill and Water Garden is designed to represent a slice of a Japanese landscape, from the mountaintops to the river beds. Muto created valleys and mounds accompanied by a rocky streambed with waterfalls, collection basins, and a shallow ford which emptied into the Swan Pond. The water traveled through its course by gravity. Among the flora used to highlight this area were various types of bamboo, conifers, Japanese maple, enkianthus, broadleaf evergreens, deciduous azaleas, and peonies. Many of these plants still survive as fine, mature specimens.

In 1912 the final Japanese addition was completed. The Overlook

Lydia Morris in Japanese attire while visiting Yokahama.

Garden was located near the entrance on the carriage road. Visitors followed a narrow path lined with stones to get to this area which was home to Oriental conifers and deciduous trees and shrubs. At the top was a stone viewing platform, constructed by Mr. Muto. Above the viewing platform a group of large stones stood watch over the area. The first stone on the east was engraved with the Japanese character for preserving loyalty and the date of the garden's opening (1912). Also present on the lower corner of this stone were carvings of the three monkeys representing the oriental proverb "See no evil, hear no evil, speak no evil." In the center of the area stood a large stone called a Fudo stone. Fudo is Japanese for immovable. This particular stone showed a Buddhist monk holding out an alms bowl carved into the base of the stone. Two more Fudo stones were located outside the garden and a third Fudo stone rested at the lower entrance to the garden. Muto also completed the Ravine Garden below the Mercury Loggia during this time.

Temple Bell by Toshiko Takaezu is popular with visitors of all ages.

Japanese Fudo stones stand guard over the garden, providing protection from evil spirits.

LOVE TEMPLE

The Love Temple was positioned to allow both the temple and its reflection in the Swan Pond to be seen from a bridge on the opposite side of the Swan Pond. Sculpted of white marble, it was modeled after the plans of Vitruvious, an Augustan student of architecture. Compared to some of the surrounding structures, the Love Temple is simple in design and plain in decoration.

MERCURY LOGGIA

The Mercury Loggia was constructed in 1913 by John Morris to celebrate the twenty-fifth anniversary of the founding of the Compton summer home. The Loggia is a small, temple-like structure constructed of Wissahickon schist with an arched plaster roof and mosaic tile floor. Located at the western edge of the English Park, the Loggia captures the feel of a Roman temple site. At the front entrance two Doric columns stand as stately guardians. Inside the Loggia is a bronze statue of Mercury, recognizable by his winged sandals. The statue is a cast of an original found near Herculaneum, a Roman town located near Mt. Vesuvius which was buried during the massive eruption centuries ago. The original work is attributed to the Greek sculptor Lysippus, or one of his students. After excavation of the town in the eighteenth century, replicas of the statue were sold around the world for $200–250.

The statue is quite unusual in several respects. Mercury, displayed as the ephebe or youthful athlete and patron of athletic contests, is pictured resting. Having a statue of Mercury, famous for his athletic speed, in a garden designed for a calm and relaxing atmosphere is an interesting dichotomy.

The Grotto beneath the Loggia is an artificial cavern created and lined with Wissahickon schist. Historically, grottos similar to this one were designed as a cool location for intellectual ponderings. A narrow winding path leads through the grotto and out into the Ravine Garden on the northside of the Loggia. Large blocks of stone were used to create the walls of the Ravine and serve as an anchoring mechanism for flowering bulbs and perennials. An artificial streambed was created to allow water to flow through the Ravine Garden and collect in a pool at the end of the path.

The Mercury Loggia, built to commemorate the 25th Anniversary of Compton.

Mercury Loggia, circa 1978, before renovation.

Mercury Loggia as renovation takes shape.

The Pennock Flower Walk features the original fountain purchased by the Morrises.

PENNOCK FLOWER WALK

One of the newest additions to the Morris Arboretum landscape is the Pennock Flower Walk, designed as a tribute to horticulturist and Advisory Board member J. Liddon Pennock and his wife, the late Alice Pennock.

The Flower Walk was placed at a site where the Morrises had elaborate flower beds, along an axis beginning at the Orange Balustrade. In keeping with the tradition of blending the old and the new, the Flower Walk combines a historical style with contemporary planting themes. The plantings that grace the Flower Walk include annuals, bulbs, perennials, and flowering shrubs.

PUMP HOUSE

Originally completed in 1908 to drain the meadow, to supply the ornamental fountains, and provide water for grazing livestock, the Pump House was restored in 1987. Restoration included work to replace the roof and woodwork and the construction of a new ten-foot diameter "undershot" steel wheel. This wheel was once fed by a fifteen-inch terra cotta pipe leading from a dam at Stenton Avenue. Today the Pump House greets visitors entering through the Northwest Avenue entrance.

Although the wheel is more for decoration than necessity today, at the time of its construction, the pump house was an integral feature. The wheel powered a three cylinder pump which pushed water uphill to a cistern in the tower of the former Compton Mansion House. The pump also provided water for the Orange Balustrade, Long Fountain, and various other water features throughout the gardens.

ROSE GARDEN

When this parterre garden was first laid out below the mansion in 1888, it contained a blending of fruits, vegetables, flowers, a few roses, and a specimen chestnut tree. To terrace the hillside, soil had to be removed from the area. This was accomplished through the use of a small train with one track constructed from the Rose Garden site to the greenhouse area below. In 1924, Lydia transformed this mixed garden into a Rose Garden. One of the most difficult tasks during creation of the Rose Garden was the construction of the rock wall. Originally the design called for the rock wall not only to maintain the slope, but to serve as a display area for alpine plants. When the stone masons constructed the original rock wall, they did a superb job without any cracks or holes in which to give plants a foothold. The garden staff attempted to remove some rocks and create spaces for plants, but their efforts caused the entire wall to collapse. Consequentially, the wall was rebuilt by the garden staff with the necessary planting spaces in place.

Elegant stone steps were constructed at the upper garden entrance. The design for these steps was copied from a similar stairway at a residence on West Highland Avenue. Roses were first planted in the 1920s, but due to a severe infestation of Japanese beetles, the Rose Garden was unable to take hold fully. Once the roses were fully established, they became a favorite of Lydia Morris. Every day that they bloomed, a bouquet of roses was carried to Compton, but only after the thorns had been removed. A guest to the mansion remarked that she did not care for roses because they were so thorny. Lydia Morris replied that her roses did not have any thorns, and proceeded to share her love of the delicate flowers with her guest.

By the mid-1960s, the Rose Garden was in terrible shape. What few rose bushes remained were infected with canker and the wall was crumbling. Restoration began in 1971. Jackson and Perkins and Conard-Pyle donated two thousand healthy roses to replace the diseased ones. Finally, a gift from the late Otto T. Mallery provided funds to fix the balustrade and install the fountain that is a current focal point of the garden.

On June 27, 1974, the rose garden was rededicated and renamed in honor of Marion W. Rivinus who had visited the Morris home on many occasions as a child. Marion Rivinus was

Step Fountain in the early days.

instrumental in many aspects of the Arboretum restoration as the first president of the Morris Arboretum Associates and a member of the Advisory Board of Managers.

Today the Rose Garden is an official display garden of the All America Rose Society. The Rose Garden is in continuous bloom from late May through October thanks to a changing blend of perennials, annuals, and woody plants along with the roses.

MADELEINE K. BUTCHER SCULPTURE GARDEN

No place in the Arboretum combines the classical and the modern with such great success as the Madeleine K. Butcher Sculpture Garden. Historically, sculptures were not unknown to the design of the Morris Arboretum grounds. From the sculpture of Mercury in the Loggia to stone lions and temple dogs in the Japanese Garden areas, sculptures have had a constant presence at Morris Arboretum.

In 1988, a Sculpture Garden was dedicated as the Madeleine K. Butcher Sculpture Garden, an outdoor gallery dedicated to changing exhibitions featuring the works of significant local sculptors.

Plans for future exhibits in the Butcher Sculpture Garden are in progress, as the Sculpture Garden is truly always changing.

"After B.K.S. Iyengar" by Robert Engman was inspired by the yoga master, who attended its installation.

"Two Lines" by internationally-acclaimed sculptor George Rickey provided a unique backdrop for a Fall Festival.

"Three Tubes" by Israel Hadany, located at the end of the Haas Oak Alleé.

"Rock Chair" by Scott Burton is on loan from Max Protech.

"Cotswold Sheep" by Charles Layland is an allusion to the English pastoral landscape which inspired the Morrises.

"Untitled" by George Sugarman.

"African Queen" sculpture, located opposite the Ravine Garden.

Children find the water pump at the Log Cabin to be lots of fun.

The Garden Railway Display, an annual exhibit enjoyed by hundreds of families, features model trains and historic replicas in the garden.

SEVEN ARCHES

The Seven Arches balustrade was built originally to serve as a toolshed for housing gardening equipment and as a pumphouse for the water features in English Park. This large structure is located on the hillside to the southwest of the English Park. The design is similar to a Roman structure from A.D. 200 called the Septizodium. The southernmost bay houses pumps which fed water to fountains and other water features around the Arboretum. The terrace and formal balustrade are constructed above the Seven Arches on the hillside affording a wonderful vista to the Wissahickon Valley.

Plant Collections

Examples of plants from the Morrises time can be seen in practically any garden area today. At the entrance to the parking lot near the old mansion site is the Bender oak (*Quercus x benderi*) which predates the Morrises and is a legacy to the longevity of oaks. Many of the extremely rare mature trees in the Arboretum represent one of only a handful of like specimens in North America. Examples of these trees include the Engler beech (*Fagus engleriana*) near the Swan Pond and the Tatar wingceltis (*Pteroceltis tatarinowii*) above Seven Arches.

In certain garden areas, the original Morris plants remain, showing the design intent of more than one hundred years ago. For example, the Japanese Hill and Water and Overlook gardens contain many of the original conifers, rhododendrons, and Japanese maples. These mature specimens make these small gardens peaceful and serene locations to visit.

The plant collection of the Arboretum is at the heart of the visitor experience. There are plants of beauty for all seasons and for all levels of garden lovers, from the beginner to the most experienced gardener. The plant collection delights and teaches and is a wonder to enjoy throughout the year.

NATIVE AZALEAS

In 1951, Dr. Henry T. Skinner traveled throughout the eastern, southeastern, and Gulf states examining and collecting a wide variety of azaleas. On his travels, Dr. Skinner recorded fourteen species, five varieties, and thirteen naturally occurring hybrids. He collected five thousand herbarium specimens and five hundred live specimens which he brought back for planting at Morris Arboretum. Although some have died, new collections are continually added. The work of Dr. Skinner has helped to provide Morris Arboretum with a comprehensive collection of the azaleas of the eastern United States.

HOLLY SLOPE

Above the Oak Alleé and below the parking lot stands an area devoted to one of the more common ornamental plants used in modern landscaping—holly. This collection was started by Dr. Henry Skinner, an avid fan of holly, when Gates Hall was added to the property in 1948. Morris Arboretum's Holly Slope is designated an official Holly Arboretum by the Holly Society of America.

ASIAN MAPLES

The Arboretum is home to a large and diverse collection of Asian maples, including many varieties of Japanese maple (*Acer palmatum*). Japanese maples come in an array of sizes and forms with beautiful spring and fall foliage. The variation in habit and leaf textures and colors make them well-suited for landscapes of any size. In addition, the Arboretum has numerous other species of maples from Asia, adding beauty to the spring and fall displays throughout the garden.❧

KATSURA TREE

Often described as the signature tree of the Morris Arboretum, this stately champion is breathtaking on any visit. Located near one end of the Oak Alleé, the impressive character of this specimen, among the largest in North America, is formed by the multiple trunks that branch near the ground. The spring bloom of this species offers masses of tiny maroon flowers and as these fade, the emerging reddish-purple leaves turn to a rich green. The fall color is an array of yellows and apricot colors and when they drop in the autumn, the leaves have a sweet smell, variously described as caramel or cotton candy. This grand specimen has adorned the Arboretum for close to one hundred years and is a great beauty to behold on any day of the year.❧

METASEQUOIA GROVE

Until the early 1940s, the 150-million-year-old *Metasequoia glyptostroboides* tree was thought to be extinct. In 1946, however, Chinese botanists found a four-hundred-year-old living tree. Seeds were sent to American botanical institutions, including the Morris Arboretum. The *Metasequoia* (or Dawn Redwood) Grove is composed of wild-collected *Metasequoia* plants raised from those seeds and planted along a small stream near the Wissahickon.

In 1999, it was dedicated in memory of Steven Murray, Vice President of Business Services at the University of Pennsylvania.❧

OAK ALLEÉ

Designed after the European Alleés (meaning "to go" in French), the Oak Alleé has undergone a great deal of change following the damage from a tornado on August 3, 1991. The original Oak Alleé was planted in the early 1900s and remained relatively unchanged until the tornado knocked down a number of the mature oak trees. The oak trees were replaced and the feature was rededicated as the Haas Oak Alleé in honor of Dr. F. Otto Haas, who was instrumental in the rebuilding of the Arboretum.❧

Volunteers are an integral part of the Arboretum in many areas. Horticulture volunteers gathered for this photo on the Magnolia Slope.

The Oak Alleé in 1967.

The F. Otto Haas Oak Alleé in 1999, after renovation.

The *Metasequoia* grove, first planted in the 1950s, is world-famous.

PLANT COLLECTION PHOTOS

The Japanese katsura tree *(Cercidiphyllum japonicum)* at Morris Arboretum, a famous specimen in the collection.

Enkianthus perulatus 'J. L. Pennock', with its namesake, is the first plant patented by Morris Arboretum.

Atlas cedar male cones *(Cedrus atlantica* var. *glauca)*.

Tabletop Scotch elm *(Ulmus glabra* 'Horizontalis') at Morris Arboretum reflects the Victorian interest in weeping tree varieties.

Edith Bogue southern magnolia *(Magnolia grandiflora* 'Edith Bogue') is an especially winter hardy selection that has been popularized by Arboretum staff.

The tea plant *(Camellia sinensis)* is the source of commercial tea.

This Engler beech *(Fagus engleriana)* at the Morris Arboretum is one of the largest specimens of this species outside of its native China.

Blue mist fothergilla *(Fothergilla gardenii* 'Blue Mist') is a blue-leaf form selected at the Morris Arboretum.

Japanese maple *(Acer palmatum* var. *heptalobum).*

Cutleaf Japanese maple *(Acer palmatum* var. *dissectum).* There are several fine specimens at Morris Arboretum that are nearly one hundred years old.

Steven Murray Metasequoia Grove *(Metasequoia glyptostroboides).*

Rhododendron 'Morris Gold' was hybridized by former curator Henry Skinner.

Black gum *(Nyssa sylvatica)*, native to the site, is an autumn favorite.

Star magnolia *(Magnolia stellata)* puts on a decorative floral display in late March or early April.

This Chinese Lacebark pine *(Pinus bungeana)* is one of the finest in North America.

Yoshino cherry *(Prunus yedoensis)* highlights one of the Japanese Garden guard stones in the English Park.

Kousa dogwood *(Cornus kousa)* produces red fruits in the fall which are relished by squirrels.

Morris Arboretum grows many kinds of witch hazel. Chinese witch hazel *(Hamamelis mollis* 'Pallida') sometimes blooms as early as late January.

Chinese witch hazel *(Hamamelis mollis* 'Princeton Gold') was jointly introduced to the nursery industry by the Morris Arboretum and Princeton Nurseries.

Katsura tree *(Cercidiphyllum japonicum)* in spring.

Katsura tree *(Cercidiphyllum japonicum)* in winter.